How to Get the Most from Exhibiting at Conferences

Shawn Collins

Copyright © by Affiliate Summit 2013

All Rights Reserved. No part of this publication may be reproduced in any form or by any means, including scanning, photocopying, or otherwise without prior written permission of the copyright holder.

Table of Contents

Introduction 1

Pre-Conference Outreach 2

Train Your Staff 3

Take a Stand 4

Have a System for Business Cards 5

Know Your Boundaries 6

Conference Meetings are Real Meetings 7

Showcase Your New Products or Services 8

Be "On" from Start to Finish 9

Stand Out from the Crowd 10

Solve a Problem with Your Give-Aways 11

Ask Lots of Questions 13

Sometimes The Best Pitch is No Pitch 14

Follow Up Immediately 15

Interactions with Booth Visitors 16

Straight Talk from Attendees on Booth Experiences 19

Introduction

Companies exhibit at conferences for a variety of reasons. Some look at the process as an expense as they seek to protect their market share.

Others approach exhibiting as an investment in their business. Those are the companies that build and maintain real relationships during and after the event.

It is essential to set measurable objectives in advance of the conference, so you can determine the ROI on your investment. Just showing up, setting up a booth, and waiting for the magic to happen is not going to cut it.

Over the ten years that we've run Affiliate Summit, we've seen thousands of companies exhibit, and there are some right ways and wrong ways to represent your company.

There are three outcomes that routinely result from having a presence at an event: hitting it out of the park with all sorts of new business and plans, maintaining a presence and achieving some branding, and then having a counter-productive experience.

You know that thing from the movie, Field of Dreams, "If you build it, they will come"? Well, that's not true. There are strategies you should apply to make the maximum impact with your booth.

In the following pages, I will share how you can make the most of your time at a conference, as well as pitfalls to avoid.

Pre-Conference Outreach

We are frequently asked how many people will be at the latest Affiliate Summit, and big numbers of attendees make the exhibitors happy in the lead up to the conference.

It makes us happy to have a crowded exhibitor area, too, because it looks nice for pictures and video. But really, it's window dressing.

You should be focusing on quality, and not quantity, and in order to get the most targeted traffic to your booth, you need to do some work in advance.

Promote your upcoming presence through your email list, social media, direct mail, and paid ads to get the word out to the right people.

Keep an eye on the list of companies attending the conference, and take advantage of any networking tools, such as apps and secret Facebook groups to arrange meetings before the conference starts.

Target the people you want to meet, and you'll make things easier for you and for them.

Train Your Staff

When everything is wrapped up with the conference and the attendees are heading home, nobody is going to remember the t-shirts and toys you gave away at the booth. They won't care about the furniture, the booth design, or anything else in the background.

They will remember the people of the company. The behavior and attitude of the company employees can make or break things for you.

Every face wearing a nametag with your company name is the company to the people visiting the booth. Those faces must keep your goals in mind and act accordingly.

It's important that everybody is up to speed on the questions they will likely be asked. Go over all issues, positive and negative, that might come up, and construct an FAQ. Use that to convey consistent answers to questions that will be coming at your team.

Take a Stand

Far too often, when I have been on the exhibit hall floor, I have seen company staff sitting down behind a table or on a couch.

Get off your butt and get out there to be with the people. If you have a table, push it back against the booth wall.

Make yourself approachable and show that you're interested.

You don't convey that impression when you're lounging around.

Your company is paying thousands or tens of thousands for you to be there for a pretty short period of time. So stand and deliver.

There will be plenty of time to sit down when you get back to the office.

Have a System for Business Cards

I keep my own business cards in my right pocket, and as I hand them to people I ask for their business card.

Also, I always have a pen on me to write notes on their card to remind me why I want to follow-up with them.

Then their business cards go in my left pocket.

I see some people use the name badge holder to store their cards or those that they receive.

Whichever way you do it, just work out some system, so you're not fishing for your business cards when you need them.

Know Your Boundaries

There is a fine line between being assertive and being aggressive.

It's assertive when you are willing to introduce yourself to anybody who walks by, and it's aggressive if you won't let a prospect leave and/or won't let them get a word in edgewise.

Be assertive at your booth.

Aggressive is best left as a cheerleader chant:

Be Aggressive
Be Be Aggressive
Be Aggressive
Be Be Aggressive
B-E-A-GG-R-ESS-IVE!

Conference Meetings are Real Meetings

Set up meetings before the conference and treat them with the same level of seriousness as you would a meeting in your office.

Get on the phone or email a good 3-6 weeks before the conference and invite key people to meet with you during the conference.

Set specific appointments for every time slot you can while you are in town to optimize your opportunities.

Make plans to get together in meeting rooms, coffee shops, and other locations when people can't get into the exhibit hall area.

Ideally, I'd suggest using a database like the Salesforce CRM to keep track of when everyone is coming to meet you. But just putting the details in your smartphone will work, too.

Be sure to follow up during the conference if they miss the appointment, so you can work out another time to do business.

Showcase Your New Products or Services

If the timing is right and you've got a launch as the conference is happening, be sure to make a big fuss about it.

Then again, the timing of the next conference is probably not in sync with your marketing calendar and your plans for the next new product or service.

However, there are a couple workarounds when the schedules do not align.

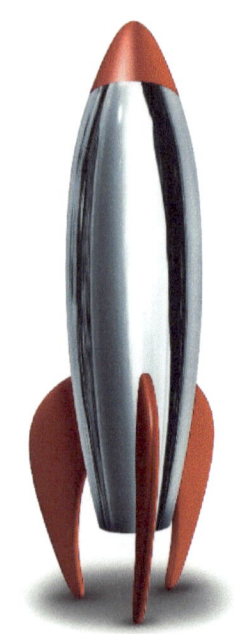

If you have released something since the last time you exhibited, make some noise about that product or service as if it were brand new. Many people are likely not aware of it, so introduce them to it at your booth.

Also, if there is something in development, you can share sneak peeks, whether they are a physical prototype or screen shots.

If you didn't launch anything in
the past 6-12 months, and you don't have anything in development, it's probably time to figure out where your customers think you can improve.

So survey anybody that comes by and build up a list of things you can work on for the future. Don't be afraid of negative feedback – embrace it.

Be "On" from Start to Finish

Working a booth for a couple days or more can be exhausting, both mentally and physically, but it's important to maintain the same level of enthusiasm throughout the conference.

Some conference attendees tend to get carried away at night and then sleep late in the morning.

Others are up early and ready for business. Be sure to be prompt at your booth in the morning and ready to do business with the clear headed and eager attendees.

Sure, the crowds get thinner towards the end, but we've heard over and over from Affiliate Summit exhibitors that the stragglers result in some of the best conversations and business, because there is more time to talk.

It's not over until the booth is packed away.

Stand Out from the Crowd

The first move in standing out at a conference is to have a good location on the floor.

In the case of Affiliate Summit, there are two ways to get the top locations: book one of the top sponsorships or secure your booth early (spots are picked in the order they are registered).

Another way to get attention is to speak at the conference. This enables you to get your name and expertise out there in both the conference program and during your session.

And when somebody from your company is a speaker, people will know where to find them or another person from the company for more information.

Great presentations and quality information are an excellent commercial for your company.

Solve a Problem with Your Give-Aways

Enough of the stress balls already. Nobody likes them, and I think you know that when you have ordered them, but you just keep doing it out of routine.

Well, just don't do it again and we're all good.

Instead, give booth visitors a product or service that solves a problem for them. Think about your various pain points at a conference and address them.

I can tell you for sure that I'll happily hear a pitch if I can get an emergency charge for my iPhone at a booth that has the cable I need.

We all see the filthy animals in the restrooms at conferences that skip out without washing their hands. Even people who were raised in barns know to wash their hands. What is this creepy behavior all about?

Anyhow, that's another problem. Solve it by giving out branded hand sanitizer.

Lots of talking leads to dry, cracked lips. I am always excited (I get excited easily) when an exhibitor is handing out some banded lip balm.

You get the idea. Just to reiterate – no more stress balls.

Ask Lots of Questions

Attendees coming to your booth want to learn more about your company, and they will likely have lots of questions.

Just the same, you should have a healthy curiosity about them. Everybody that steps up could be a future, lucrative partner in business, so treat them that way. Find out who they are, what they want, and how you can work together.

Also, it's useful to ask questions to determine if that person in front of you is a competitor who is fishing for information. Ask for a business card. Sure, some people don't bother with them, but spies most likely won't have one, either.

And do they have their nametag stashed away or turned around. That could be a red flag that they are trying to hide their identity.

Sometimes The Best Pitch is No Pitch

The Always Be Closing scene in Glengarry Glen Ross is great. It's one of my favorite scenes in any movie ever.

But that doesn't have to be the approach when you are working a booth.

Get a feel for the person you are chatting up, and figure out if they might be more than a potential partner for you. They could also be a friend.

After all, business thrives on relationships, and it makes things happen easier if you're friends with people.

It's totally OK to talk about sports, music, movies, or whatever at the booth. There are people I do business with where it's more than a transaction. It's a pleasure.

I tend to do more business with them.

Follow Up Immediately

You can't follow up too soon.

If there is downtime on the exhibit hall floor, start organizing business cards and leads right there. Finish this up in the hotel room later on.

This way you can actually fill holes in your meeting schedule while you are still at the conference.

Sometimes that is not possible, so get the business cards organized and follow up that night with an email and/or LinkedIn connection, and then a phone call the next day.

When you get back to the office, break out a pen and some thank you cards for some hand-written notes. Trust me, they have a nice impact.

Interactions with Booth Visitors

A couple of years back, we ran an article in FeedFront Magazine titled "Properly Pitching Your Network at Affiliate Summit" by Robert Adler.

He shared his thoughts on various interactions he had at booths that turned him off from working with the companies he was interested in.

This article is focused on the affiliate marketing space, but it transcends to other sectors, as well.

Here is what he had to say…

The one aspect of an Affiliate Summit that always gets brought up is the gifts and/or items, commonly known as "schwag," that companies give out in the exhibit hall.

This is usually what will be discussed for at least a week after the show, and will be remembered until the next show. However, one aspect that is overlooked is how the affiliates were treated when they approached the booth.

Here are a few simple tips that will be helpful for both new and seasoned affiliate managers.

1. Do not look at someone's badge right off the bat. Try asking for their name, instead of immediately looking for a first name and color on the bottom of their badge. It usually helps when you consider that they are an individual, instead of just "person number 384." Sometimes, I walk up with my badge turned around backwards just to prompt them to ask me who I am. Just a quick side note to the person with the bar-code gun trying to snipe me as I grab one of your business cards… nice try.

2. If you are in the middle of a conversation with an affiliate, and see someone behind them, please do not walk away, mid-sentence, to talk to that person. It is extremely rude, and the affiliate will spend the rest of the day telling how "they walked away mid-sentence – forget about them," when asked what they thought of your company.

3. Never judge a book by its cover. This may sound like common knowledge, but I chuckle whenever I see affiliate managers give more priority towards someone wearing a suit and tie over a person wearing a t-shirt and shorts. This tip does not just apply to clothing. I am going to go out on a limb here, and say that if you have been to a conference before, you have, more than likely, spoken to a drunken attendee, who is so far gone; they have forgotten their own name. A good rule of thumb is to talk to them sober, before you consider whether they are an asset to your company.

4. Every network swears that they "have the highest payouts and most exclusives." At the risk of going off on a tangent, I do not care if you are brokering the offer. If the conversion rates are comparable, and so are the payouts, the only thing that matters to me is the quality of service by my AM (Affiliate Manager) and the company. When you are willing to help me, my loyalty resides with you, and that is the bottom line. If you want to hook affiliates for long-term, instead of just having them run one offer and then drop you, make sure you stress the point that you will actually help them make their business more successful. Remember, loyalty is important in business practices and works both ways.

If the examples above sound familiar, I'd highly recommend you change the way you deal with affiliates. You'll find it's better for your paycheck and your network.

Straight Talk from Attendees on Booth Experiences

There was a session at Affiliate Summit a couple years ago with candid advice on representing your company at conference from past attendees.

Here are the speakers from that session...

- Tricia Meyer, Owner, Sunshine Rewards (Moderator)
- Robert Adler, President, The Link Builders
- Ad Hustler, Chief Hustler, Ad Hustler, LLC
- Kim Rowley, Owner, Key Internet Marketing, Inc.

The panel originated from Robert Adler's article in FeedFront Magazine titled, "Properly Pitching Your Network at Affiliate Summit."

The article resulted in so much discussion that we decided to bring Robert Adler together with a few other folks in the industry to further discuss how to best represent your company at a conference.

The following is a summary of the panel discussion.

If you would like to watch the video of that session, it is available to view for free on YouTube – you can find it at: http://affsum.it/booth-tips.

Don't Look at Their Name Tag – Introduce Yourself

ROBERT ADLER: Very simplistically, if you go up to a booth or you're working a booth, someone comes up to you, please for the love of God, don't look at their name tag to get their name. Ask them for their name, because you'd be surprised how many people will actually just go straight for the name tag, but then you scan and see, "Oh, they're not an affiliate, they're an agency. He's not that important or he's a network instead of an affiliate. Oh, he's not that important."

Always go after who they are first, because you never know what they're going to do a year from now, two years from now, six months from now, a month from now. The person that is working for a network now might be an affiliate tomorrow. You never know. The fastest way to kind of set things of in the wrong direction is to assume that they are something that they are right now, instead of what they might be in a week, two months, six months, whatever it maybe.

More importantly, just introduce yourself. Business is supposed to be personal to a point, so don't go off from just what they're handing you. Go off and actually get to know them; it will help you out in business a lot better.

TRICIA MEYER: You will find that a lot of people who are here wear different hats, so it maybe that their tags says that they are merchant, but they actually also has some affiliate sites, too, or vice versa, so there are a lot of people here that do a lot of different things at the same time.

Don't Look Over Their Shoulder for Someone Better

TRICIA MEYER: What about when you're standing and you're talking to someone and they start looking over your shoulder like they are waiting for the next person to come up behind you?

AD HUSTLER: I don't like that. I actually had that happen once with a company. I think it was at Affiliate Summit. The guy, he's really rude, I don't know why he's rude to me. I don't know. He started talking to somebody else while he's in the middle of talking to me. I remember after that, the guy wanting my business, I told him, "You're rude to me." I was like, "I'm not going to do business with you." He's been pursuing I think for the last six years. He's trying to do business with me ever since, I'm still not wanting to talk to him.

TRICIA MEYER: You may feel like you're just looking over our shoulders too, assess the traffic, see how many people are waiting in line so you can hurry up the conversation, but to us it feels like you're looking for someone more important to talk to rather than talking to us in that moment.

KIM ROWLEY: I have to admit the ones that look at my name badge quick, I don't even bother to talk to them, because I think it's rude.

Never Judge a Book by Its Cover

ROBERT ADLER: A lot of people especially if it's your first time here, even if just looking out, you can kind of see it. Some people will dress up in a full suit, some people will dress up in a bottom down, some people just really don't care, and then others will do what I do, which is pretty much a t-shirt and shorts.

Never think that the way someone dresses equates to how much money they make, or how much they can help you, or what they can do for you, because that's probably the number one thing that lies the most. No one ever really gets that if it's their first time here, but after that they slowly learn over and over and over again that it does not do anything to equate to your skill level, what you do, how you do it, or anything in between.

I've met people that literally will walk around in a t-shirt and shorts, or walk around in something a lot more casual than that, that make a lot of money doing what they do, but no one even knew that time of day, because they think that they're not serious, or anything along those lines. Never judge based on that. Always get to know them for who they are.

KIM ROWLEY: I agree with the gender bias. I still think a lot of some CPA networks are, they go towards the men not the women thinking the women can't drive the leads, but we can.

AD HUSTLER: I know nobody would expect that somebody would think that I would not be professional. The truth is, I may not look professional, but I'm probably one of the most professional people that you could deal with, so don't judge the book by its cover.

TRICIA MEYER: Mine is a little bit different. I tend to get the "You must be the PR Person for the business or are you here to hand out treats or something like that?" I actually get, "You're either one that does the SEO and the programming, and can we talk to somebody else in your company, the owner or something like that?" That is me, me, all of those things.

So yes—you never know who is it that you are talking to, it can be really be offensive if you assumed that they are the assistant, if you assumed that they're just there working in the booth and it could turn out that they are the owner of the company and you completely ruined your chances of working with them.

Don't Make False Claims about Your Business

TRICIA MEYER: Has anybody ever heard one of the networks say that they have the highest payouts or exclusives that no one else has, because that seems to be kind of a big pitching point? We're actually looking through the exhibitor guide. We're not going to name names, but you all know who you are, you 7,500 out there that all have the highest payouts. 99.9 percent of you must be lying.

AD HUSTLER: I agree. It's very obnoxious, the highest payouts, the best offer, all that kind of nonsense. The truth is any affiliate network can get pretty much any offer, and any affiliate network can get most any price, and they can make up the price anyway, because they can just scrub the leads. The price doesn't really matter how much they're paying out on the lead, it's more about the relationships.

I have affiliate networks that I like to work with and I really don't care necessarily what the payout is that they're putting out on the street or what offer they have, because I could always just ask them to get the offer I need at the price I need, and it's either going to covert as well as where I'm running it somewhere else or not, so it's just all nonsense.

Develop a relationship with an affiliate, make them trust you, do right by them and it won't really matter if you have the best payouts or the highest, the best selection of offers or whatever it is, because you're going to have that relationship regardless. They're going to come back to you every time. No other networks are going to be able to steal them by saying they have a better payout on some dating offers or something, so maintain the relationship.

KIM ROWLEY: I agree. In fact, I'll run some offers that pay less just because I like the network that they're on, and I know that I'm going to get paid. I like the relationship.

Differentiate Yourself from the Competition

TRICIA MEYER: We were kind of playing a little game before we started here going through the exhibitor guide and Rob was reading off the descriptions of the companies. It was amazing to me that company after company, when he read the description, I couldn't tell you who it was because every description sounded the exact same.

If what you're pitching sounds the exact same as the people next to you, the next booth over, no one is going to remember who you are. You have to pitch to us what it is that's different. You may think using those buzz words about exclusive and highest and percentages and things like that are different, but the reality is that those are the exact same things that all the other people that we talk to this week are going to say to us.

There has to be something that's unique about you, whether it's unique about you as a person. If it's unique about your company, about where you're located, your mascot, whatever it is that's unique about you, that's what you have to get across to us, because those are the things that we're going to remember when we get home and we're flipping through all those business cards and throwing 99 percent of them away.

Booth Babes

TRICIA MEYER: Name one thing that we'll make you walk passed an exhibitor faster than anything else?

KIM ROWLEY: Booth Babes! Not so much that they are not nice to look at, it's that they don't know what's going on, what if you have a question about the company, but they hired somebody to stand, some pretty gal to stand there to hand out cards, what if you have a question and she has no idea about your company to answer any of your questions.

AD HUSTLER: I am going to agree on the booth babes. I have other things that annoy me too. I like looking at hot chicks as much as anybody else, but I really just don't need them in an Internet marketing convention, because unless they can answer some questions that I have to ask. I just find it obnoxious. They look pathetic to me. You're not going to attract any true performer with the booth babe. I don't think, because if they're true performer they can buy their own girl, they don't need to walk over here and look at the ones at your booth. I wasn't joking.

Show Interest in Your Own Product or Service

AD HUSTLER: I really hate when people that are working at the booth look disinterested. I can remember I think it was last Affiliate Summit East, I guess, and there were somebody like an old looking chap sitting in at a booth like sitting on the highest chair with his legs cross reading a newspaper. I'm like, "I'm not going to approach your booth and I'm just not interested in whatever it is that you're selling if you're not interested in what you're selling." I need to see your excitement for me to get excited.

Don't Be Aggressive

TRICIA MEYER: I don't like that aggressive like sales mentality of trying to put something in my hands to get me to talk to you, when you're standing there and you think, "If I can get her to hold on to the pen or hold on to whatever, then I got her standing here and talking to me." That might work in retail sales, but that doesn't work in affiliate marketing. It's a different ball game.

If I see people that are standing there and I see them doing that to other people, I kind of scope out the aisle, and if I see those people that are standing there like trying to get you to take the magazine, so they can get you hook and then reel you in, I'll cover up my badge and run really fast passed them so that they don't have to stop.

Because I don't want to feel trapped. I want to feel like you're approachable or you as a person approachable. If you're sitting at practice for lunch, whatever, I don't want to feel like you're trying to trap me, because if you're having to trap me then it probably means whatever you have isn't interesting enough to make me want to stay without that.

Know Your Product or Service

<u>AD HUSTLER</u>: I think that knowledge is the best sales tool at a conference like this. Not really "salesy" kind of things, because everybody here is a sales person when you're really think about it. When everybody here is a marketing person and knows how to sell, they can spot like cheesy sales guy staff from mile away, but if you're knowledgeable and you can answer questions about your product and make me really educated about what you're selling and make me interested, that's the best sales tool you're going to have.

Don't Spam Business Card Email Addresses

KIM ROWLEY: Don't spam me. On my business cards, I use a specific email address, so I know that it's from my business cards and I cannot believe how many lists I get added to with that email and instantly that's a turn off that I don't want to do business with you. But if you want to send a follow up email like, "Hey, I meet you at Affiliate Summit." That's fine.

TRICIA MEYER: I think that's a really important point about the follow up, something that we don't have a place to talk about in any other place, but the follow ups afterward today. Obviously, you're going to meet people today, tomorrow is Tuesday and there's going to be that travel time of Wednesday, Thursday.

I think if I don't end up following up with somebody, usually within a week, maybe, of when I'm in a conference, that person falls way to the bottom of the list, and I end forgetting about the conversation that we had, or something else becomes more important at that time.

So you have to continue that pitch though, not incredibly aggressively like emailing and emailing and calling until they respond, but at least that initial, "Hey, we meet at the Affiliate Summit, this is what we talked about." A little reminder to me about what we talked about, then I'm more likely to be able to take the time to work with you after that.

Standing Out on the Exhibit Hall Floor

KIM ROWLEY: I think a good example of being different would be not necessarily the swag, but let's says all of your people wore green capes, and then you either handed out green capes, so you followed up and you said in your thing, "Hey look for us in the green capes and then maybe you even want to send the green cape later." It's like "Oh, I remember them." You want to be memorable.

Bad Experiences at Booths

TRICIA MEYER: Let's talk bad experiences. Anyone had a bad experience at the booth that you'd like to share?

ROBERT ADLER: I got one. For the exhibitors that purchased the ability to use the little scanner gun on your pass, don't snipe me as I'm walking down the aisle. I'm not even joking like, "She must have been paid on commission or something for everyone that she scanned." But she was literally just standing. They're going like this and just scanning every single person walking down the aisle. She must have like 6,000 email address at the end of that, but that's why I now block the scanner code. The scanner gun  can be probably one of your best assets if used correctly, but if you don't use it right, I won't even stop at the booth. That is just pathetic. At least, that's my opinion.

AD HUSTLER: I don't like when I get to a booth and when I decided to actually asked a question or talked to somebody and they can't tell me what they do quickly. I just want to hear what you do quickly. I don't need to talk to you for half an hour. Sometimes, these guys they won't let you go and you just have to almost get rude with them to leave. I think that you just got to be respectful of people that are walking around, of affiliate's time and make sure that you're just getting your point across and letting them go, not trapping them at your booth, unless they want to be trapped at your booth, but they'll stay there though.

TRICIA MEYER: I think the worst experience I ever had was someone who trapped me at their booth, and what they did had nothing to do with what I do. There was no way that we could work together, but they kept me there for like a good ten minutes going on and on and on, and finally at the end when I could get a word on edgewise, I kind of indicated, "I told you what I do and you told me what you do and we have no synergy or anything, whatsoever." He said, "I know, but I'm really new to this so I'm trying to practice my pitch."

AD HUSTLER: Try it on someone else.

TRICIA MEYER: I just thought, "Oh, all right. Thanks though. There's the ten minutes gone and your name is mud." There is a level of honesty to have with the people that you're talking to, if you don't know the answer to a question, even if it's about your own company, you want to be honest about that and say you'll get back about that, but that's something you don't know that the person asked. There is a certain level of honesty that you want to have, so that you can start building that relationship. I think also in some cases, there can be a little bit too much honesty.

AD HUSTLER: To her point about the questions, if I asked a question, I want an answer. I want an answer to the questions that I asked, not an answer to whatever your agenda was to tell me about. I don't think most of the companies here could actually answer a question, when you asked them a question, because they just go off talking about whatever it is they want to talk about and you're disinterested. If asked a question, answer that question. That's it.

Good Experiences at Booths

TRICIA MEYER: Being the sunshine girl that I am, let's go positive. What are some good experiences that you've had with companies pitching you, either over lunch, or at the booth, or something like that at conferences?

What are the things that have been good, like meeting somebody that made you follow up with them afterward?

AD HUSTLER: Usually for me, if somebody is intelligent, I really feel like they know what they're talking about, and they're an expert in whatever it is that they do makes me want to work with them, because it gives me confidence that I can learn something from them or that I'm working with the best. If they are some random affiliate manager and affiliate network, I don't have a lot of confidence, but if you're well known affiliate manager, and if you're telling me things that I don't know, and they sound like they're interesting. You really have to pique my interest and sound educated. If you don't sound educated, you're done with me. I want you to be the expert of whatever it is you do. I don't want to know more about what you do than you do.

TRICIA MEYER: For me I like when the person who's pitching their company to me isn't just pitching their company to me, but they are listening to what I'm saying about my company, so that we can start brainstorming together off of that. You met that person at lunch and they tell you what they do and you say what you do and they say, "You know what? We have this then maybe we could together on it." They say, "Tell me more about this."

And you can tell that they're actually listening to you. You can tell that they're listening to what you're saying, and what your business model is and their mind, they're thinking how to put those pieces together and you can work together. By the time I leave that conversation, I'm energized about that relationship and I'm thinking this is somebody that I really want to follow up with, because now in my head I've already gone to the next level, not just I will follow up and exchange business cards.

I'm thinking, "Yes, I could launch that. I could put that on my site. I could blog about that." That will be something that would be great for my company. That is something that my members would love. As we're having that conversation, and I know that you're interested, truly interested in me, because you see a possible business relationship between us, you can really feel that from people.

KIM ROWLEY: I have a shoe blog and so when people ask me what my site is, I say, "I have a shoe blog." and if they have a shoe client, "Can we send you a pair of shoes to review? Plus, we offer this commission and we'll give you a higher commission for higher placement." Yes, so then when I get the shoes in the mail, I'm definitely going to blog about them.

ROBERT ADLER: Mine is very simplistic—just don't lie to me. It's honestly just that easy. If I sit down with someone for lunch and at the end of the lunch they literally look at me and say, "I cannot think of one way that we can work together." Okay, cool. I'll take your business card and when you can think of something when I shift into another niche or something, I'll make it happen, because I trust you and you didn't lie to me and say, "We can bring that in. We can do that for you. We can do this. We can do that."
Meanwhile, he's thinking at the back of his head, "I have no idea where you get that offer. Or I have no idea where to get that product. I have no idea what company I could bring in for him." Whereas, at the same time, I'm sure down the road I will be doing something that will go with whatever they have. My big thing is don't lie to me. If you're honest, I'll work with you eventually, but if you're not honest, I will never work with you, ever.

About Affiliate Summit

Affiliate Summit was founded by Missy Ward and Shawn Collins in 2003 for the purpose of providing educational sessions on the latest industry issues and fostering a productive networking environment for affiliate marketers.

Get details on the next Affiliate Summit event at
http://www.affiliatesummit.com

www.ingramcontent.com/pod-product-compliance
Lightning Source LLC
Chambersburg PA
CBHW040927180526
45159CB00002BA/638